Community BUILDERS

Jesse Jackson

Jesse Jackson

I Am Somebody!

by Charnan Simon

Children's Press®
A Division of Grolier Publishing
New York London Hong Kong Sydney
Danbury, Connecticut

Photo Credits

Photographs ©: AP/Wide World Photos: 16, 18, 29, 31, 41, 44; Archive Photos: 32; Black Star: 26 (Bob Fitch), 20 (Charles Moore); Corbis-Bettmann: 12; Courtesy of Sterling High School: 10, 13; Folio, Inc.: cover (Drew Harmon), 45 (Matthew McVay); FPG International: 24; Impact Visuals: 21 (Diana Davies), 28 (Jason Lauré), 37 bottom (Rick Reinhard); Photo Researchers: 7 (Will & Deni McIntyre); Photri: 37 top (Lewis), 3, 9, 35; Reuters/Corbis-Bettmann: 8; Time Magazine: 2, 19, 39, 43 top (Bruce Talamon); University of Illinois, Sports Information Office: 14; UPI/Corbis-Bettmann: back cover, 17, 23, 43 bottom.

Author photograph ©: Tom Kazunas

Library of Congress Cataloging-in-Publication Data

Simon, Charnan.
    Jesse Jackson : I am somebody / by Charnan Simon.
       p. cm. — (Community builders)
    Includes bibliographical references and index.
    ISBN: 0-516-20291-X (lib. bdg.)   0-516-26133-9 (pbk.)
    1. Jackson, Jesse, 1941-   —Juvenile literature. 2. Afro-Americans—Biography—Juvenile literature. 3. Civil rights workers—United States—Biography—Juvenile literature. 4. Presidential candidates—United States—Biography—Juvenile literature. I. Title. II. Series: Simon, Charnan. Community builders.
E185.97.J25S56 1997
973.927'092
[B]—DC20   96-42193
                                               CIP
                                             AC

Contents

Chapter ONE

With Liberty and Justice for All

What would you do if you thought you were being treated unfairly at home or in school? What if your brother got to sit in the front seat of the car and you always had to sit in the back? What if some children in your class got brand-new books, and you had to use an old, torn paperback? What if you always had to play on the side of the playground without any swings? Would this be fair? Would it be "liberty and justice for all," like it says in the Pledge of Allegiance?

6

**The Pledge of Allegiance is a promise
to be loyal to the United States.**

The United States is a democracy. A democracy is just about the most fair kind of government there is. In a democracy, there are laws to protect the civil rights of citizens.

But even in a democracy, things are not always fair. Sometimes the laws protecting civil rights are broken. Sometimes those laws might even be changed.

Civil Rights

Civil rights are the freedoms that are shared as members of a national community. Citizens of the United States have the right  to vote. They have the right to say what they like and write what they like. They have the right to practice whatever religion they believe in. They have the right to be treated fairly by the government and by other citizens.

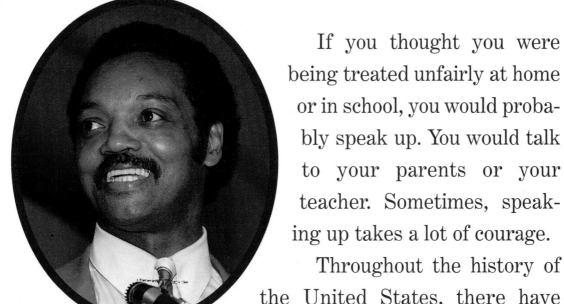

Jesse Jackson

If you thought you were being treated unfairly at home or in school, you would probably speak up. You would talk to your parents or your teacher. Sometimes, speaking up takes a lot of courage.

Throughout the history of the United States, there have always been courageous people who have spoken up when things were not fair. Some of these people lived long ago. But some are alive right now.

One of these people is the Reverend Jesse Jackson. Jesse Jackson has been a civil rights worker all his life. As an African-American, he has worked especially hard for African-American civil rights. But Jesse Jackson believes that all the members of a community—rich and poor, black and white, men and women, young and old—deserve to be treated with respect. He has spent his whole life trying to make our country a better place for all Americans.

"Promise Me You'll Be Somebody"

When Jesse Jackson was growing up, his Grandmother Tibby always told him, "You're as good as the next person, and don't you forget it. Promise me you'll be somebody!"

Jesse wanted to believe his grandmother, but sometimes it was hard. Jesse was born on October 8, 1941, in the quiet little town of Greenville,

Jesse as a young boy in South Carolina

10

South Carolina. In those days, it wasn't easy for an African-American child to feel as if he were as good as the next person—especially if the next person was white.

African-American children couldn't go to the same schools as white children. They couldn't attend the same churches. They couldn't play in the same playgrounds or eat at the same restaurants. They couldn't even drink from the same drinking fountains.

Segregation

Although slavery ended after the Civil War (1861–65), segregation, or separation based on race, did not. When Jesse Jackson was growing up in South Carolina, there were many laws that forced black people and white people to lead separate lives.

Water fountains labeled "For Colored Only" were a common sight throughout the segregated South during the 1950s and 1960s.

In spite of segregation, Jesse had a mostly happy childhood. He was always a leader in school. He did well in both his studies and sports. He loved going to church. Sometimes he even got to speak from the pulpit, just like a minister. But it

12

always bothered Jesse that everywhere he went, white people seemed to get better treatment than black people.

After Jesse graduated from high school, he went "up North" to college. He had earned a football scholarship to the University of Illinois and was looking forward to playing quarterback. But Jesse soon found that segregation existed even in

After Jesse graduated from high school, he enrolled at the University of Illinois.

the North. There weren't any written laws to keep African-Americans and whites separated the way there were in the South. But there were plenty of unwritten laws.

Jesse ran into the first of these unwritten laws on the football field. Although he was an excellent quarterback, he was not allowed to play that position at the

University of Illinois. The quarterback was the leader of the team. It wouldn't look right for an African-American quarterback to lead his white teammates.

Jesse didn't like not being able to play quarterback. He didn't like other things about his school, either. Black students and white students lived in different houses. They could go to the same classes, but not to the same social events. After a year, Jesse decided to move back to the South.

Although there were no laws to keep Jesse from playing quarterback for the University of Illinois football team, he was not allowed to play.

Chapter THREE

The Young Activist

In 1960, Jesse Jackson transferred to the mostly black North Carolina Agricultural and Technical College (A & T) in Greensboro. It was an exciting time to be at A & T. Many students there were becoming famous in the civil rights movement for their lunch counter sit-ins.

There was a department store in Greensboro called F. W. Woolworth. African-American customers were welcome to shop at Woolworth's. But they were not welcome to eat at the Woolworth's lunch counter. The A & T students didn't think that was fair. They

The Civil Rights Movement

African-Americans have struggled for equal rights since the Civil War ended in 1865. During the 1950s and 1960s, this struggle grew stronger and more organized. It became known as the civil rights movement. The civil rights movement did much to end legal discrimination against African-Americans.

Most civil rights marches were peaceful demonstrations in support of equal rights for all citizens.

In 1960, African-American college students sat
at the Woolworth's department store lunch counter.
They refused to leave until they were served.

staged a protest. Every day they went to Woolworth's and ordered food. When the owner wouldn't
serve them, they kept on sitting at the counter. They
brought schoolbooks and studied. They didn't cause
trouble, but they didn't leave, either.

Day after day, more black students came to sit at
the counter in peaceful protest. Soon white college
students joined them. Eventually, the Woolworth's
owner gave in and let anyone, black or white, eat at
the lunch counter.

Even though Jesse Jackson (center) was arrested for leading civil rights protests, he didn't give up his goal of equal rights for black Americans.

Jesse Jackson agreed with what these A & T students were doing. He quickly became a leader in the Greensboro civil rights movement. Jesse organized eat-ins in restaurants. He organized sleep-ins at hotels. He organized watch-ins at movie theaters and wade-ins at swimming pools. Once he even went to jail for his beliefs. But—slowly—segregation in Greensboro began to end.

18

After Jesse graduated from North Carolina A & T, he moved to Chicago, Illinois, to attend the Chicago Theological Seminary. Jesse still wanted to help African-Americans win their civil rights. But he also felt a strong desire to serve God. Jesse felt that, as a preacher, he could help African-Americans and serve God at the same time.

By that time, Jesse had a wife, Jacqueline, and a baby daughter named Santita. The young family didn't have much money, but they were happy in Chicago. Jesse studied hard, and he always kept up with the civil rights movement.

Jesse, with his wife Jacqueline

In 1965, civil rights workers were trying to change the laws that made segregation legal in the South. To do this, they encouraged African-American citizens to vote for political candidates who would support new laws that would end discrimination.

19

The Southern Christian Leadership Council (SCLC) helped black people understand the sometimes confusing voter-registration forms that were required for citizens to be able to vote.

But in many parts of the South, it was hard for black Americans to vote. Black citizens had to pay high taxes and take difficult tests before they could vote. Sometimes they were threatened, or even beaten up, when they tried to vote.

A civil rights group called the Southern Christian Leadership Council (SCLC) was trying to change that. Led by Dr. Martin Luther King Jr., members of the SCLC traveled all over the South helping black Americans vote.

In March 1965, the SCLC planned a march from Selma, Alabama, to Montgomery, Alabama, to publicize their voter registration drive. Jesse Jackson organized a group from Chicago to join the march.

20

During the 1960s, Jesse was a forceful speaker at civil rights marches.

Dr. Martin Luther King Jr.

Dr. Martin Luther King Jr. was an African-American Baptist minister, and the leader of the civil rights movement in the 1950s and 1960s. Dr. King was awarded the Nobel Peace Prize in 1964. Although Dr. King preached non-violence, he was murdered on April 4, 1968.

Chicago

Chicago, Illinois, is located in the midwestern United States, along the shores of Lake Michigan. It was founded as a city in 1837 and today is home to more than three million people.

Jesse made quite an impression in Selma. In his usual take-charge way, he quickly began giving speeches and telling marchers what to do. Some of the older SCLC leaders didn't like that. They wanted to know who this bossy twenty-three-year-old from Chicago was!

But Dr. King liked Jesse Jackson's energy and intelligence. Dr. King liked Jesse so much that he gave Jesse a special job to do when he went back home.

Chicago was not a good place for African-Americans to live in 1965. Many black families were very poor. It was hard for them to find jobs because

A run-down Chicago neighborhood during the 1960s

A black woman protests a New York City shoe store's failure to employ black workers.

most of the stores and businesses in Chicago were owned by white people. Many whites wouldn't hire black workers. They wouldn't buy products that had been made by black-owned companies. Without good jobs, African-American families couldn't afford decent housing. They lived in crumbling apartments located in dangerous neighborhoods.

With the SCLC, Jesse Jackson started an organization in Chicago called Operation Breadbasket. Operation Breadbasket's goal was "to bring bread, money, and income into the baskets of black and poor people." Through Breadbasket, Jesse hoped to strengthen Chicago's black community.

"What we need to do is simple," Jesse told his friends and neighbors. "If a store doesn't hire hire black people, don't shop there. If a store doesn't sell products made by black companies, don't buy the products it does sell. Boycott those stores—refuse to shop there!"

Jesse's boycotts worked just the way he thought they would. When black families stopped shopping at stores that didn't treat them fairly, the stores lost

Jesse Jackson's emotional sermons encouraged
listeners to speak out for equality.

money. Store owners didn't want to go out of business. They began hiring more black workers. They also began selling more products made by black-owned companies.

Sometimes Jesse worked as many as sixteen hours a day on Operation Breadbasket. But he also found time to preach at the Chicago Theological Seminary. Every Saturday morning at 9:00 A.M., Jesse delivered a sermon full of energy that offered hope and inspiration to anyone who wanted to listen. Soon so many people wanted to listen that Jesse had to move to the Capitol Theater in downtown Chicago to speak.

It was at these Saturday morning meetings that Jesse began his famous "I am somebody" chant. "I am somebody!" he would call out to the crowd. "I may be poor, but I am somebody! I may be uneducated, but I am somebody! Respect me. Protect me. Never neglect me. I am somebody!" Proudly and loudly, the crowd would call back, "I am somebody!"

The year 1968 was a sad time for Jesse Jackson and other civil rights workers. On April 4, 1968, on a motel balcony in Memphis, Tennessee, Dr. Martin Luther King Jr. was shot. Jesse was there when Dr. King died.

African-American youths around the country rioted the night that Dr. King was killed. Angry and upset, they roamed city streets, throwing rocks and bottles and destroying property. Jesse immediately returned to Chicago to try to calm things down. "I am calling for nonviolence in the homes, on the streets, in the classrooms, and in our relationships, one to another," he said. "I'm challenging the youth of today to be nonviolent as the greatest expression of faith they can make in Dr. King—put your rocks down, put your bottles down."

Black youths steal merchandise from a Chicago store during the riots that followed the 1968 assassination of Martin Luther King Jr.

Jesse, as the head of Operation Breadbasket, led many civil-rights protests. This one took place in 1969 at the mansion of Indiana governor Edgar D. Whitcomb.

Jesse Jackson continued working for Operation Breadbasket after Dr. King's death. But he and the other SCLC leaders didn't always agree on how things ought to be run. In 1971, Jesse resigned from the SCLC.

FOUR

Pushing On

Jesse Jackson left the SCLC, but he didn't leave the civil rights movement. On Christmas Day, 1971, Jesse formed a new organization called PUSH. At first, PUSH stood for People United to Save Humanity. Later, Jesse changed it to stand for People United to Serve Humanity.

PUSH had many of the same goals as Operation Breadbasket. Jesse was still committed to helping African-Americans get better jobs, better housing, better health care, and better schools. Within a year, there were PUSH chapters in sixteen cities, with more than sixty thousand members.

As Jesse traveled around the country with PUSH, he visited many schools. He was disappoint-

As the leader of PUSH, Jesse Jackson spoke out in favor of better job opportunities for black workers.

Jesse Jackson's PUSH-Excel program encouraged
students to study hard, to believe in their abilities,
and to stay away from drugs and alcohol.

ed with what he saw. There were too many young African-American students who were not studying. They were experimenting with drugs and alcohol. They didn't seem to know how to talk to their parents or teachers.

Jesse wanted to help these young people. He started PUSH for Excellence (PUSH-Excel). PUSH-Excel was Jesse's way of challenging African-American students to strive for excellence in everything they did. Tirelessly, Jesse traveled to inner-city schools across the nation. He told students to work hard and to believe in themselves. "There is nothing more powerful than a mind made up," he said. "Make up your mind to do better, and you will. You are somebody!"

Jesse asked students to sign a contract for him. He wanted them to promise to study for two hours every night. He wanted them to stay away from drugs and alcohol. He also encouraged parents and teachers to stay involved in the children's lives.

In 1983, Jesse was back in Chicago for a very important election. A man named Harold Washington was running for mayor. If Harold Washington was elected, he would become the first African-American mayor of Chicago.

Jesse worked hard on Harold Washington's campaign. He traveled throughout the city giving speeches about what a good mayor Mr. Washington would be. Jesse helped thousands of African-American citizens register to vote. He told everyone—black or white—how important it was to get involved in the election. When Harold Washington won the election, it was in large part because of all of Jesse Jackson's hard work.

Jesse campaigned tirelessly in support of Harold
Washington's successful bid for mayor of Chicago.

Chapter FIVE

Running for President

After the Chicago election, Jesse decided to get involved in politics in a bigger way. He thought that he could help all of the people in the country. He decided to run for president of the United States in the 1984 election.

Jesse wanted all Americans to feel that they had a voice in his presidential campaign. He wanted to speak up for people, especially blacks, that he felt had been left out of American politics in the past. Jesse called his supporters the Rainbow Coalition.

36

Jesse Jackson's campaign for president drew many supporters, but he did not win the election.

Jackson's Rainbow Coalition welcomed many diverse people who supported equal rights for all Americans, regardless of racial background.

Shirley Chisholm

Jesse Jackson was not the first African-American to run for president of the United States. In 1972, an African-American congresswoman from New York named Shirley Chisholm was defeated in her bid for the presidency.

Many people thought from the beginning that Jesse Jackson's campaign was hopeless. But even though he did not win, he came in third out of eight Democratic candidates. He helped register more than two million new voters. He made people all over the country think about what it really meant to be an American.

After the election, Jesse continued his work with PUSH and PUSH-Excel. He also spoke out for fairness and justice around the world. He visited Africa and the Middle East. He fought against apartheid in

Apartheid

Apartheid was a system of government in South Africa that separated the races. Even though there were more blacks than whites, the whites had all the power. Apartheid finally ended in 1991. The first elections open to both blacks and whites were held in April 1994.

Jesse has become known throughout the world
as a leading voice in support of the poor.

South Africa. He became an informal spokesman for
downtrodden people around the globe.

When Jesse wasn't traveling, he could still be
found delivering Saturday morning sermons back
home in Chicago. By then, he and Jacqueline had
five children. Santita and her brothers Jesse Jr. and
Jonathan were in college. Only Yusef and little
Jacqueline II still lived at home. Jesse was a devot-

ed father and frequently took one or more of the children with him when he traveled.

By 1988, Jesse was ready to run for president again. He still wanted his Rainbow Coalition to provide a voice for America's forgotten people. He still campaigned for better housing, better education, better jobs, and better health care for all Americans.

Jesse Jackson's campaign to win the Democratic nomination for president was bigger and more organized than his 1984 campaign had been. Jesse finished in second place in the Democratic primaries. He won more than seven million votes.

Primary Election

A primary election is a contest in which voters choose the candidates who will represent each political party in the general election. In the United States, two main political parties hold primaries—the Democratic Party and the Republican party.

Jesse Jackson, center, with the candidates for the 1988 Democratic presidential nomination: (from left) Gary Hart, Michael Dukakis, Bruce Babbitt, Richard Gephardt, Paul Simon, and Albert Gore.

But Jesse Jackson did not win the nomination. Some people said it was because he didn't have enough political experience. Other people said that the United States just wasn't ready for an African-American president.

Whatever the reason, Jesse Jackson proved that an African-American could be taken seriously as a presidential candidate. He offered great hope to the black community in the United States. And people of every color believed in his message of civil rights and justice for all.

Jesse Jackson is still working hard to bring better opportunities to all Americans. He continues to speak out on civil rights issues around the country and throughout the world. He still delivers Saturday morning sermons whenever he is in Chicago. PUSH and PUSH-Excel still spread their message of hope and encouragement. And the Rainbow Coalition still supports political candidates who share Jesse Jackson's belief in civil rights for all.

Perhaps one day Jesse will be a presidential candidate again. But even if he isn't, he has worked hard to make the United States a better place for all Americans. "We have a great nation," Jesse Jackson has often said. "But it can be made greater if all Americans are included."

Jesse is still an active
supporter of equality, justice, and
excellence for all Americans.

In Your Community

Jesse Jackson has devoted his life to making the United States a better place for all Americans. What can you do to make your community a better place?

Can you take cookies to your local polling place during the next election? Ask an adult to help.

Can you write a letter to your congressperson or senator, tell-

Timeline

| 1941 | 1959 | 1960 | 1962 | 1963 |

1959 — Jesse enrolls at the University of Illinois.

1962 — Jesse marries Jacqueline Brown.

1941 — Jesse Jackson is born on October 8 in Greenville, South Carolina.

1960 — Jesse transfers to North Carolina A & T; he becomes a leader in the student civil rights movement.

1963 — Jesse graduates from A & T; he enrolls in Chicago Theological Seminary.

ing about what you think should be done to make your community a better place? Your librarian can help you find the correct addresses.

Martin Luther King Jr.'s birthday is a national holiday. Does your community do anything special to celebrate this day? Ask your parents or teacher how you can take part.

Jesse meets Dr. Martin Luther King Jr., and is put in charge of the SCLC's Operation Breadbasket in Chicago.

Jesse resigns from the SCLC and organizes PUSH; he runs unsuccessfully for mayor of Chicago.

Jesse makes a second unsuccessful bid for the Democratic party's nomination for president.

1965 — **1968** — **1971** — **1984** — **1988**

Dr. Martin Luther King Jr. is murdered in Memphis, Tennessee.

Jesse runs for the Democratic party's nomination for president of the United States; he establishes the Rainbow Coalition.

To Find Out More

Here are some additional resources to help you learn more about Jesse Jackson, PUSH, and the Rainbow Coalition:

Books

Haskins, James. *I Am Somebody! A Biography of Jesse Jackson.* Enslow, 1992.

Hatch, Roger D., and Frank E. Watkins, eds. *Straight from the Heart.* (Essays by Jesse Jackson). Fortress, 1987.

McKissack, Patricia C. *Jesse Jackson: A Biography.* Scholastic, 1989.

Otfinoski, Steven. *Jesse Jackson: A Voice for Change.* Fawcett Columbine, 1989.

Wilkinson, Brenda. *Jesse Jackson: Still Fighting for the Dream.* Silver Burdett, 1990.

Organizations and Online Sites

National Association for the Advancement of Colored People (NAACP)
4805 Mount Hope Drive
Baltimore, MD 21215
http://www.naacp.org/

National Rainbow Coalition
1700 K Street, N.W.
Suite 800
Washington, DC 20006
http://www.cais.net/rainbow/rchome.html

Rainbow/PUSH Coalition
930 E. 50th Street
Chicago, IL 60615

Index

About the Author

Charnan Simon lives in Madison, Wisconsin, with her husband and her two daughters. She is a former editor at *Cricket* magazine, and sometimes works at a children's bookstore called Pooh Corner. But mainly she likes reading and writing books and spending time with her family.

Ms. Simon lived in Chicago, Illinois, for many years. She remembers how vigorously Jesse Jackson campaigned for Harold Washington in 1983 and is proud to have cast her vote for Mr. Washington.